Farmers' Markets

The UK Potential

Farmers' Markets

The UK Potential

Alan Chubb

éco-logic books

First published in 1998 by éco-logic books

éco-logic books is an imprint of Worldly Goods

Worldly Goods publishes and distributes books that promote practical solutions to environmental and social problems. For further information contact:

Worldly Goods
10-12 Picton Street
Bristol BS6 5QA

ISBN 1 899233 04 0

Photographs   Alan Chubb
Design and typesetting   Jon Carpenter
Cover design   Deborah Morris and Helen Miller Designs
Printing and binding   Doveton Press, Bristol

Contents

Acknowledgements

The research for this book was undertaken as part of the Soil Association Local Food Links project, which promotes and supports local organic food production. The project is funded by the Department of the Environment, Transport and the Regions' Environmental Action Fund.

The opinions stated are those of the author and do not necessarily reflect the opinions of the Soil Association.

Kalamata, Greece. Farmers' market

1 Farmers' markets and their benefits

Farmers' markets are markets where producers themselves bring their produce for sale direct to the public. No bought-in goods are allowed to be sold. This type of market is not new, but in recent years has been superseded by the shopping mall with its out-of-town supermarkets as well as a change in the more traditional street markets away from local produce to wholesale products and supermarket reject goods.

A farmers' market is where the public can expect to find quality produce that is fresh and wholesome and sold at a fair price. The idea is to provide local small-scale producers and processors with a forum in which to sell direct to the consumer and thus contribute to the economy of the community in which they live.

Festival and music events associated with these markets help create an atmosphere that is vibrant and fun, and that will make shopping a sociable and enjoyable activity.

This study has been written in order to review the existing models of farmers' markets and to investigate how they may be adapted and established in the UK as part of a strategy to develop local food links.

What are the benefits of farmers' markets over existing types of markets?

To the producer

- Direct selling, avoiding middlemen, gives good returns to producers. This is in contrast to wholesale fruit and vegetable markets which exist to give retail shops a central location where they can buy daily or weekly. The costs of running the market and the wholesalers' costs must be borne by the producer and the retailer who passes on their costs to the consumer. The difference between the producer prices and retail prices can be substantial. In a price study covering 358 items in 15 farmers' markets in the USA the overall price of produce was 34% cheaper than at the local supermarket.[1] This price difference is thus available to the producer to share between himself and the consumer as he sees fit.

- Cash flow is regular. When selling to the wholesale or retail trade, business accounts are normally settled monthly. A smallholder operating on a tight cash flow margin needs cash to purchase small but critical inputs for his smallholding.
- Producers get direct customer feedback on their produce and prices which allows them to improve their service to the consumer. They can also introduce new lines and get immediate reactions. There are hidden benefits as producers can advertise other local retail outlets where their produce is available.
- The need for transport and packaging of goods is reduced; hence costs are reduced.
- There is less wastage in outgrades that might be required when selling through supermarkets.
- small-scale producers gain an outlet for their produce as they are unable to supply in any large quantity.

To the community
- Revitalises village, town or city centres. Successful markets attract people back into town centres so that other shops can benefit.
- Provides a social meeting place. People who live locally are especially attracted to these markets where they can informally meet their neighbours in a friendly open situation and where children can be entertained in a safe environment.
- Encourages social interaction of people from different walks of life especially between urban and rural dwellers.
- Allows producers working in isolated conditions to meet directly with their customers and other producers.
- Provides access to fresh food and so improve diets for local people. Farmer markets can supply 'food deserts' in inner city areas where fresh food retail outlets have cease to trade.
- Gives a marketing opportunity for those on low incomes or others with the need for greater flexibility in working hours who wish to start up income generating activities.

To the local economy
- Increases employment and can boost trade for adjacent retailers.
- Attracts business at times when trading may not normally take place.
- Encourages farming diversification.
- Encourages consumers to support local agriculture and local businesses.
- Gives an opportunity to encourage Local Exchange and Trading Systems (LETS).

To the environment
- Reduces transportation of goods, hence reducing 'food miles' and fossil fuel use.
- Reduces vehicle pollution and noise.
- Encourages more consumer friendly production practices e.g. organic or pesticide-free production.
- Encourages farm diversification and hence biodiversity.
- Helps raise awareness of sustainable development and the links between society, the economy and the environment.

These benefits can be seen to be influential in the development of farmers' markets in the USA as reviewed in Chapter 2. American experience indicates that specific farmers' markets will generate some of these benefits but not all, depending on their specific location and the function that interested participants actually want the markets to fulfil.

Kalamata, Greece. Farmers' market.

2 Existing models

Until recently there have not been any true farmers' markets (where only local producers sell their own produce to the customer) in regular operation in the UK. However this type of market is well established in the USA and other European countries.

Farmers' markets in the USA

Farmers' markets are based on a tradition of smallholders producing to sell directly to the local town. These traditions go back over 200 years in the UK and the USA when, for example, the Central Market in Lancaster, Pennsylvania opened (see below). However the development of the supermarket and out-of-town shopping malls in the USA during the 1930s meant a decline in interest in these types of market. The supermarkets could offer the benefits of:

- self service: allowing customers to inspect and handle the produce before buying.
- shopping convenience: goods for sale were all pre-packaged, labelled, priced and well displayed.
- one-stop shopping: all the shopping could be done at one place with a car park alongside.
- economies of scale: as bulk purchasing of goods for a chain of supermarkets was possible, prices to the customer were lower than in the local shop.

During the late 1980s consumer concern over food prices, quality and health/food issues stimulated interest in buying fresh fruit and vegetables directly from the producers.

• •

Growth of farmers' markets in the USA

	1976	1994	1996
No of markets	100	1755	2400

In 1995 over 30,000 farmers were selling at farmers' markets.
Total value of produce sold is $0.7billion a year.
1 million consumers visit farmers' markets each week.
90% of customers live within 7 miles of the markets.
New York State had 170 farmers' markets in 1994.

Source: USDA Farmers' Market Survey Reports 1995 and 1996.[2]

• •

There are four main types of farmers' markets in the USA :

1 The small urban or rural parking lot market with an average of 16 smallholder farmers selling their produce on trestle tables to 350 consumers with a minimum of preadvertising.[3]

2 The urban market with an average of 34 growers selling to 2,000 consumers/day.[3] These markets are often part of a group of markets that operate at different sites on different days within a large city and have a central organising group or manager.

• •

The New York City Greenmarket

This organisation runs 25 markets at 18 sites within 3 boroughs of New York. About 150 farmers sell at these markets to approximately 40,000 customers/week. The markets are the sole retail outlet for 70% of these farmers. It is estimated that these markets keep 8,000 acres of land near New York in active production. Only goods produced by the seller are permitted to be sold, as the main purpose of the markets is to support local farmers.

Source: *Connections: Creating urban space.*
The Bruner Foundation 1991.[4]

• •

3 The large permanent urban market that operates more than one day/week with a large number of stalls catering for over 5,000 customers/day.

● ●

The Central Market, Lancaster, Pennsylvania

This old established farmers' market has up to 10,000 consumers/day buying from over 200 stalls The market is housed in an old brick building dating back to 1889. It is owned and operated by the City of Lancaster. Stalls are rented annually with vacant licences being auctioned. No sub-letting is allowed and the stalls must be used solely for the sale of food products and farm produced goods.

● ●

4 The ethnic markets where immigrant populations congregate to sell locally produced ethnic foodstuffs that are not normally available. An example is the Vietnamese Market in Washington.

Farmers' markets in Europe

The selling of fresh produce in Europe has mainly taken place in traditional street markets, which have been in decline in recent years.[5] There are, however, still more than 6000 weekly markets, for example, in France representing 8% of total food sales nationally.[6] The importance and popularity of the 73 fresh food and open air markets of Paris is such that they receive an annual subsidy of £2.3 million.[13] These markets are dominated by commercial traders as in the UK and producer sellers find it necessary to identify themselves as such. Markets in Germany are less important as fresh food outlets with only 3,000 market events/year compared with the 300,000 in France.[7] There are also similar permanent covered markets as found in the USA and UK.

● ●

Kalamata farmers' market, Greece

This is a traditional market centred in the old part of the sea port of Kalamata in the southern Peloponnese. The market operated each day in a square that overflowed from a covered permanent fruit and vegetable market. After an earthquake in 1987 the immediate area was destroyed and a new purpose built market was erected at a site nearby. The market is divided into equally sized sections selling meat, fish, fruit and vegetables and producer only sales.

•   The buildings are 95% owned by the Local Council and 5% owned by shareholders. In 1996 the market generated a profit of £110,000.
•   There are 450 stalls for food sales of which 150 are permanent shops.
•   The farmers' market operates on Wednesdays and Saturdays.

- Rents for farmers' stalls are £22/month.
- Average turnover is £330/stall/week (£210 on Saturdays and £120 on Wednesdays).
- In order to qualify for a stall, the producer must be inspected by the local council agricultural inspector whose responsibility it is to verify that the goods on sale are produced by the farmer himself.
- Sellers travel up to 100 kms to get to the market and also sell to other similar but smaller markets in the area.

There are concerns that the advent in the last five years of large supermarkets in Kalamata has started to squeeze the profits of the permanent stallholders. The market manager has found it hard to convince these stallholders to take a more aggressive advertising and selling approach. The farmers' market sellers however have been unaffected so far by the supermarket competition.

• •

Ludlow Food and Drink Fair.

3 Markets that currently operate in the UK and their major constraints

The types of markets outlined below have all been successful at times. None of them can be considered true farmers' markets where producers only sell direct to the public. The question is whether any or all could be used or adapted to accommodate the farmers' market concept or whether these will only prosper if established from scratch.

1. Street markets

These markets are commercially run by private companies throughout the UK. There are 17 major marketing companies in the National Association of Private Market Operators but there are in fact more than 300 full time or part time unaffiliated operators. The markets sell a range of goods including fruit and vegetables as well as clothing, hardware, shoes, prepacked and fresh meat and cheese. They operate on different days so that traders can travel to different markets in the region and sell goods throughout the week. Charges for stalls are variable according to what is being sold. Typically the charge is £2.40 – £2.60/ft to sell fruit and vegetables. The trader has to supply all necessary selling equipment including the stalls. These markets operate from approximately 9.00am to 4.00pm.

The major constraints are that these markets are perceived by the public as places where shoddy low quality goods are sold, although bargains can be found. The organisers need to make the market as large as possible in order to maximise stall rentals. Little concern is paid to the balance of goods, other than ensuring that as large a range of goods as possible is on sale. There is no quality control and no guarantee that the seller will return the following week to accept returned goods. As the emphasis is on cheapness, the quality also tends to suffer especially with fruit and vegetables. Because these markets operate mostly without cover there can be wide fluctuations in stall turnover depending on the weather, especially in winter. Stallholders selling fresh produce run the risk of losing unsold stock. This will especially hurt the smallholder whose main selling advantage is the freshness of produce. If it is not sold at the market he will lose the premium prices by having to sell on the wholesale market the following day.

• •

Glastonbury Street Market: the sellers' day

6.30am: The day starts for Tam and Lucy whose job it is to sell the produce from Radford Mill Organic Farm at the commercially run Glastonbury Street Market. The produce has been harvested the afternoon before and kept in cold storage overnight and now must be loaded into the back of the farm truck.

7.00am: They are on the road to Glastonbury with a short stop to deliver a 'veggie box' to their accountant in Wells.

8.00am: They unload the produce and set up the trestle tables. The vegetables are well displayed, not in old vegetable field boxes but with rustic baskets and trays.

8.30am: The stall is ready for the first early buyers.

The other stallholders are selling a wide range of goods from cheap hardware and plastic imported toys to secondhand clothes. There are two other non-organic fruit and vegetable sellers, whose produce comes from the wholesale markets. Typically the organic vegetable prices are 25-30% higher than the non-organic produce. This doesn't deter the customers who come to buy at the stall for the freshness and flavour of the produce as well as its organic status.

The stall is well known and has its regular customers. Tam and Lucy greet them all by name and that even includes the dogs of the customers.

2.00pm: Sales have died down now after a lunch time rush. The special offers board that is posted on a nearby pillar is rewritten, offering special prices for items that are left over.

3.00pm: A stock taking is made of the little unsold produce in order to assess total volume of sales.

3.45pm: The stall is dismantled and unsold produce is packed back into the truck.

4.00pm: Travel back to Radford Mill.

4.30pm: Unloading of the truck and a relaxing cup of tea in the garden where the day's takings are calculated. The day's turnover was £326 at a cost (transport,wages,site rent etc.) of £75.

• •

2. Annual festivals

These are markets that are organised either by national or local organisations in conjunction perhaps with local authorities. There is a theme celebrating either a national or local day. For example, Common Ground have successfully promoted National Apple Days in conjunction with local authorities.

The major constraint is that because they are infrequent or one-off events, they do not justify the planning of production to supply them. However, they do promote locally produced food and raise public awareness of the range of produce that is available. This in turn could stimulate the formation of a farmers' market.

• •

Ludlow Food and Drink Fair

This market festival has now been operating for three years. The idea was started by the Chamber of Commerce in Ludlow as a way to extend the tourist season and to show the public the range of local foods that is available. The festival takes place over a weekend in September (Friday evening to Sunday evening) and is divided into two parts:

a. *The Street Market*. This is modelled on a farmers' market and is held in the main square of Ludlow. It is not restricted to producers only. There are approximately 30 stalls erected for the event with awnings and tables supplied. The sellers pay £20/stall. There is no restriction on what is sold as long as it is food or drink orientated. Thus there are cooking utensils, cookery books and locally made table cloths for sale as well as the local cheeses, meat pies, yogurts, fruit and vegetables (both organic and non-organic) cakes and sauces. Live folk music helps to give the occasion a festive air.

b. *The Food and Drink Marquee*. A separate entrance fee of £1.00 is payable to cover the legalities of selling alcoholic drinks. There are 34 stalls erected within the tent selling and offering samples of locally made beer and wine. There are also further processed food stalls who offer free samples to complement the drink.

• •

3. Covered markets

These are permanent markets that are located in central town locations and are normally owned and controlled by the local town or city council. They are typically operated under a deed of charter, sometimes dating back over 200 years. The Exchange Market in Bristol is a well established example of this type of market. There are permanently erected stalls, as they are enclosed within a building that is secure. Because of the permanent nature of these markets, the stalls are in fact small shops that operate in the same way as any small high street shop except that the rent is cheaper (£400/yr at Bristol). A full range of goods is on sale, as can be found in the high street, including fruit and vegetables from both local and wholesale sources. Craft shops and specialist food shops are also present. Some markets offer special days for temporary stallholders to sell local and imported goods or foodstuffs. The Pannier Markets of North Devon are a special case of this type of market.

The major constraint is that these markets are given over to permanent stallholders with little space for low cost temporary stalls. Customers are offered the same goods that are available in local shops, albeit sometimes at slightly lower prices. Many of these markets have recognised the need to revitalise their business and have looked at novel ways of attracting the public back into the market areas. The organising of one day events such as 'French Markets' or food fairs are such examples but one-off events like these, whilst successful in bringing customers for the day, do not ensure regular custom. Some markets have certain allocations of areas for local producers but coordinated efforts to bring in new sellers have either not been successful or not followed through.

Most of these markets are local authority owned and run and cannot operate as an independently run market business as income generated from the market is returned to the authority. There will always be the problem of underinvestment in these established markets.

Old charters governing some city markets state that no other market can be established within 6 - 7 miles. This could restrict the siting of a new farmers' market in the area unless existing stallholders agree to waive these rights.

• •

Barnstaple Pannier Market

The Pannier Market operates in an old vaulted central market on Tuesdays, Fridays and Saturdays. The market place is used on other days for antique sales etc. Priority is given to producers but not exclusively so. It is traditionally the market where the farmer's family visits the nearby main cattle market and the wife sells the home produce.

There are 450 stalls available (4ft frontage). They cost £90 -£103/year depending on three price zones. There are no permanently erected stalls. Stalls are rented annually and there is little change from year to year. In the three years to 1997, only 45 stalls have changed hands. 150 stalls are allocated to non-foodstuffs such as leather goods, clothes, antiques and bric-à-brac. The remaining 350 stalls are for local producers who come from a 15-25 mile radius around Barnstaple. The commercial traders, however, come from as far away as Bristol and Somerset and follow different markets on different days. The market is run by a professional manager who is employed by the North Devon District Council. He is in control of stall allocation and is keenly aware of the importance of keeping the balance of local producers and commercial non-food traders in order to maintain the market atmosphere. Advertising of the market is low key and is directed at the tourist trade. The market made a profit of £250,000 in 1996.

Spitalfields Organic Market

This market was established in 1992 in the old covered wholesale Spitalfields Market building in central London. The market was established as a private business as a way to promote and bring organic food to the centre of London. It was a great success in the first weeks with 30 organic stalls. Early advertising concentrated on promoting the organic aspect of the market although other regular stalls continued selling a range of normal street market goods. After the first three months the number of traders dropped to about 12 but has stayed constant ever since. It took 18 months before traders' takings covered their start-up costs.

The reason for the drop in numbers of traders has been the cost and distance that producers have to travel into central London as well as the fact that the organic market only operates on Sundays; this is not popular with farmers as produce must be picked fresh on Saturday and packed ready for transporting to market early on Sunday morning.

Currently there are six traders who are producers themselves and who also buy organic goods from other suppliers, and six who are wholesale buyers and sellers of organic produce from as far away as Stroud and Gloucester. The market has served as a spawning ground for new organic producers and processors.

• •

4. WI Markets

There are 528 Women's Institute (WI) markets grouped into 70 co-operatives operating one day a week throughout the UK. They are organised by WI Country Markets Ltd. representing 48,000 shareholders. The markets operate in local community halls, selling home produced goods including baked and processed foodstuffs and craft work. Goods are sold by volunteers (who staff the stalls). A commission of 8%–20% is charged by WI Country Markets Ltd. The markets have an average turnover of £100,000 ranging from £12,000 to £500,000. The company is a non-profit making organisation and charges are to cover costs only.

WI Markets actually operate a type of farmers' market in that all produce is locally grown or produced and they have gained an excellent reputation for quality. Because of the small volume of produce per supplier they have to operate as a market co-operative with volunteers selling the produce and not the producers themselves. There is great scope for WI Markets to become involved in farmers' markets, since they already have the experience in organising local markets, in handling foodstuffs and meeting environmental health regulations and requirements.

The constraint on WI markets is that they are unable to expand due to their dependence on volunteer sellers, but they are successful in giving small-scale producers and processors a cheap retailing outlet that could be used as an interim option or as an integral part of a farmers' market.

5. Wholesale markets

These are commercial markets that operate daily to supply bulk fresh produce from producers and importers to the retail food industry. New Covent Garden supplies not only London retailers but also fruit and vegetable outlets throughout the UK. Class 2 fresh produce from these markets can be found in the street markets mentioned above.

The main constraint here is that these markets mostly cater for medium to large-scale producers requiring reasonably large volumes of crops to be harvested at a time. Lower wholesale prices are offered. Transport costs are high as these markets are centrally located in only a few large cities.

Bath Farmers' Market

4 Who are interested in establishing farmers' markets?

The success of the US farmers' markets has been due to the benefits that such markets have on a wide range of local interests. Experience in the USA as well as in the UK has shown that interest comes from the following groups and organisations:

1. The farmers themselves

With supermarket buyers dominating the fresh produce wholesale markets, farmers have few marketing alternatives. Hence they must gear their production to supply these outlets and so are committed to medium to large-scale monocropping to produce the uniformity, quality and volume of produce that the supermarkets want. Smallholders are normally unable to participate in these types of markets. Moreover, farmers find that the necessary farming production practices are not easily sustainable and disrupt their overall farm production planning. Small- to medium-scale farmers especially are thus keen to develop more flexible alternative retail outlets. Those with farm shops and 'pick your own' have already developed the necessary retailing skills and a move into a farmers' market is an easily managed step.

Organic farming produces healthy, untainted food as well as increasing local employment, and so farmers' markets offer a unique opportunity for organic producers. Customers at these markets are looking for quality food that is fresh. They come because they are interested in what they eat and are concerned with possible agrochemical contamination of fruit and vegetables and especially meat. Farmers' markets appeal to this kind of shopper as they can buy direct from the producer and can question them about their production practices. The presence of certified organic produce and 'unsprayed' chemical-free produce is thus what customers expect, and successful market managers need to actively encourage these producers.

Organic producers in the UK have in the past encountered problems with the normal fruit and vegetable retail outlets as they do not get their produce promoted properly and the premium prices that are being asked are not perceived by the public as being justified.

Organic smallholder production systems entail the growing of a wide range of crops rather than just a few, hence it is hard to produce the volume required for the wholesale markets. For this reason direct marketing outlets such as 'veggie boxes' have been developed. Marketing organic produce at farmers' markets also overcomes these problems as well as offering some advantages over the box schemes.

Farmers' markets offer a special market for produce from farms that are 'in conversion' (farms that are currently undergoing the three-year changeover to organic status and eventual certification). The produce from farms 'in conversion' may not get the full premium of certified organic produce but will be preferred by farmers' market customers to regular fruit and vegetables.

• •

Barnstaple plant seller

Derek specialises in rare and unusual garden plants which he started to produce for sale at his smallholding farm shop near Barnstaple. When the Barnstaple by-pass was constructed he lost most of his passing trade and so started renting a stall at the Barnstaple Pannier Market on Saturdays and Wednesdays. He also attends a similar market at Bideford on Thursdays. At first he also sold his plants at outdoor street markets and car boot sales but has given these up as they are too dependent on the weather and too downmarket, with customers expecting to pay very low prices. He now spends all his time selling at markets in the south west and as far away as Birmingham and London. His wife concentrates on the production side. They also have a mail order scheme.

He pays £165/year at Barnstaple for each 3ft table that he uses (normally 5 tables) He considers that an income of at least twice the stall price is the minimum required to continue renting the site. Other markets he sells at charge 10% of sales.

Derek has adapted his production to suit the Barnstaple clientele by for example increasing the numbers of bedding plants on sale at the beginning of the summer. There are four other plant sellers in the market but there is no direct competition as each stall sells different types of plants.

Derek is well aware of the advantages of this form of selling, quoting the opportunity to meet and talk with prospective buyers and advise on plants in general. He also is able to display a range of plants, especially any new lines that he has.

● ●

2. Community development organisations

Farmers' markets are suited to small-scale producers as there are minimal marketing costs. The establishment of a farmers' market locally can encourage existing producers and offer new producers a marketing outlet which will thus stimulate the local economy. There is an opportunity for community development organisations to work with individuals and groups to initiate small-scale production of vegetables or crafts to supply new farmers' markets. The promotion of city farms, community gardens and allotments and subscription farming all enable people to:

- produce their own food
- utilise vacant land
- give unemployed and underemployed people a chance to develop skills, self confidence and income-generating possibilities by producing for a specific market.

• •

New Farmers New Markets Project

Since 1989 the US State Depts of Agriculture and Health have promoted farmers' markets in New York City to assist low income households at nutritional risk. Food coupons were issued to 42,000 families which were redeemable at the farmers' markets, generating $600,000 in sales.

After the initial success it was apparent that there were not enough farmers' markets operating and many poorer areas were unable to benefit. Despite the availability of funding new markets could not be successfully established as there were too few farmers supplying the farmers' market network. Thus the New Farmers New Markets project was initiated through working partnerships with the State Depts of Agriculture and Health and seven community based organisations to train and instruct groups of adults and youth in fruit and vegetable production on land allocated by interested organisations (such as the Mission Society). In the last two years a total of 56 people have taken up small-scale farming on a total of 18 acres. This has allowed the establishment of a further two large farmers' markets as well as fostered business skills and opportunities for those involved.

Source: *Cornell University Coop Extension Funding Proposal* 1994.[8]

• •

3. Government social services

Social services departments in the USA have seen the establishment of farmers' markets as an opportunity to ensure better nutritional diets for those families at risk.

A feature of many poor inner cities is the lack of shops where fresh food can be purchased. Thus in the USA the issuing of food stamps does not necessarily alleviate the nutritional problems as there is nowhere to purchase fresh vegetables. Farmers' markets are low cost alternatives to encouraging supermarkets back into deprived areas. Furthermore fresh fruit and vegetables can be made available to food stamp recipients through vegetable box schemes run from farmers' markets.

In the UK the 'New Deal' programme under the Welfare to Work initiative promoted by the Department of Education and Employment gives the young unemployed a choice of work in an environmental task force, an employment or voluntary sector placement or training. There would be scope in this programme to promote the production and processing of farm products in community programmes or even with placements in local food businesses supplying farmers' markets. Training in horticultural, processing or marketing skills could also be an essential part of this programme.

• •

Community Food Security Programmes in Los Angeles

In 1996 the Los Angeles City Council introduced a food-security ordinance that allocated $280,000 to supporting projects that work towards making fresh produce available to all residents. For example projects are funded that purchase and package produce at farmers' markets for delivery to low income families, thus helping to increase the customer base of the local farmers' market. This is not a donation-based hunger programme but an effort to educate and build relationships within communities and between farmers and consumers.

Source: *In Search of Food Security*, M. Newman 1997[9]

• •

4. Local businesses and chambers of commerce

Inner city areas and town centres have lost their traditional bustle with out-of-town hyperstores attracting shoppers with 'all under one roof' shopping. Thus there are fewer casual buyers frequenting the centres of towns where small-and medium sized retail outlets are found. By establishing farmers' markets in these areas customers are attracted back into the town centres to the benefit of stores surrounding the markets. The Marin County farmers' market at Vallejo in California USA which recorded over 5000 customers/week found that local business sales went up by 38%.[20] In the UK the Ludlow Food and Drink Fair was established especially to maintain the town as a tourist attraction into the late summer season.

● ●

Syracuse, New York

In 1973 the Syracuse Chamber of Commerce assisted in the establishment of a farmers' market as a means of revitalising the urban centre. A street was blocked off every Tuesday during the summer as a location for the market. After one year there were 12,000 visitors/day to the market and local businesses reported sales increases of 8 - 14%. This had a snowball effect on improvement in the local area. Free bus services to the market were established and picnic tables were sited on a nearby green area. Even the politicians came to set up tables at election time as it was a good place to meet potential voters.

Source: *Public Places and Spaces*, R. Sommer 1989[10]

● ●

5. The environmental lobby

This covers a range of groups including Friends of the Earth, Transport 2000, SAFE Alliance, and the Women's Environmental Network. The predominance of the supermarket in the retail food industry and their policies of central processing and packing and 'just in time stocking' has meant a substantial increase in the transport of food around the UK. SAFE Alliance has coined the term 'food miles' to raise awareness of the distance food now travels before it arrives at our local supermarket.

● ●

A vegetable grower in Wales sells through two outlets in his local town. Produce sold through the greengrocer travels from the farm to the shop, where it is bought by the consumer: total distance 5 miles. The same produce sold through the supermarket goes 5 miles to the packhouse, then almost 100 miles to a distribution centre in north-west England, nearly 100 miles back, and then to the consumer: total distance almost 200 miles.

Source: *The Food Miles Campaign*, SAFE Alliance.

● ●

In order to reduce this dependence on transport these organisations want to encourage the idea of sustainable local food economies which promotes patterns of local production and consumption. By producing and selling food locally at farmers' markets, not only is the cost of transport and environmental pollution reduced but the income from food sales also stays within the local economy. This is especially important in smaller town communities.

6. Organisations that represent producers

In the USA, farmers' markets are organised as non profit associations or as community services. State agricultural extension services have played a major part in the important aspect of recruiting and assisting small-holder farmers' market participants in production and marketing advice.

In the UK, the Agricultural Development and Advisory Service (ADAS) offers consultancy assistance to individuals and groups of farmers who would like to develop alternative markets as part of a diversification programme. This involves liaison with organisations such as the Farm Retail Association and National Farmers' Union to give guidance and advice on sourcing of national or European Union funding (e.g. Objective 5b funding which is an EU initiative to help diversification of rural enterprises). The Farming and Rural Conservation Agency (FRCA) is also actively supporting alternative marketing initiatives.

• •

Proposed Knowsley farmers' market

An attempt to establish a farmers' market in Knowsley near Liverpool was carried out in early 1996 by the Groundwork Trust and ADAS/FRCA in conjunction with the local council. The initiative came out of a study of the opportunities for agricultural development of the hinterland of Liverpool carried out by ADAS. The local council recognised the need to revitalise the area concerned as there was a lack of fresh retail outlets. There was also interest from farmers in the hinterland of Liverpool who needed new retail outlets.

A potential site at the Ravenscourt car park was identified and a series of three meetings were held with interested farmers. 20 - 25 farmers attended the first meeting but fewer attended the subsequent meetings as many thought the potential site was unsuitable. The farmers who continued to show interest were from North Wales and Lancashire, and not local. As the minimum group of 12 farmers could not be found the market did not go ahead.

Concern was expressed that inadequate custom would be found in the area; it was also felt that the siting of the market was in an area where customers would expect low prices and low cost food. Further market research was needed. Producers had not been given time to assess their production plans to supply the market and the organisation of the market was too rushed. Participants also thought it important to assess whether the project should be seen as an agricultural development project or as a social development project. This would have important consequences when approaching funding agencies.

ADAS, working with Groundwork, have subsequently been asked by MAFF and the local community to take another look at establishing farmers' markets, along with other methods of direct selling of vegetables in the area using Objective 1 Funding.

• •

The Soil Association has developed the Local Food Links project to encourage the local production and sale of both organic and non-organic food. This involves many different direct marketing and production initiatives in order to achieve a sustainable local food economy. The promotion of farmers' markets is an important aspect of this programme. These markets have been seen to be popular with organic producers and consumers in California, USA where 55% of farmers' markets had certi-fied organic goods for sale.[14] By selling organic produce at a farmers' market the producer can command premium prices in a niche market (in addition to the savings gained in direct selling) where customers come specifically to get quality, fresh and chemical-free fruit and vegetables.

7. Local authorities

The Local Agenda 21 initiatives that are now established in the UK are mandated to review the environmental sustainability of both local government policies and local community and business practices as a whole. This includes the role that local food production and marketing can play in the development of both urban and rural economies. The reduction of 'food miles', the stimulation of sustainable rural enterprises and regeneration of inner cities are an integral part of this important initiative. A number of local authorities are actively involved in considering the establishment of farmers' markets as part of the Local Agenda 21 initiatives and Bath and North-East Somerset have already organised a pilot project of three farmers' markets during September–November 1997.

● ●

Bath farmers' market

In early 1997 the Bath and North-East Somerset Council Local Agenda 21 office, in conjunction with the Bath Environment Centre, decided that a farmers' market would not only help local growers find a retail outlet but also supply the growing demand locally for good quality fresh fruit and vegetables. The University of London Wye College who had been advocating a similar market in Kent gave the initial impetus.

A part time market manager was recruited and a series of three producer-only farmers' markets were organised for Saturdays in September, October and November 1997. A list of local producers was compiled and contacted in conjunction with the Bath Organic Growers and similar local producer organisations. The first market was a great success with 24 producer stalls selling fruit, vegetables, fresh and processed meats, plants and cut flowers and baked goods from the local WI and others. Over 3,500 customers were recorded at the first market followed by 5,000 at both the second and third markets. A fourth market for December 1997 was added to the programme so that a fully self financing market could be held to test the feasibility of holding these markets on a regular basis in the future.

Lessons learnt were:

- The importance of good publicity and the raising of public awareness of the role that this kind of market can serve.
- The location in a covered but underused existing market place near a leading supermarket store meant that there was a guaranteed number of casual visitors that were frequenting the supermarket as well as those drawn to the market by supportive press TV and radio coverage.

- Local traders welcomed the presence of the market as it brought more people to an otherwise underutilised site.
- Local producers responded favourably to a new retail outlet.
- The public appreciated fresh good quality produce and wished to support these local enterprises.
- Producers are generally conservative and can be reluctant to test out new markets if the costs are high. Thus initial underwriting of start-up costs is important.

Full details of the Bath farmers' market experience have been published separately by éco-logic books.

● ●

8. The consumers

In the UK 15% of household expenditure is on fresh produce[4] and vegetables are the fourth largest item in the weekly food bill (fruit is sixth). This represents a total expenditure of over £6 billion (1991 figures). Weekly expenditure per person on vegetables in 1992 averaged £1.82 and £1.06 for fresh fruit. Thus there is a huge market that farmers' markets can exploit. Consumption of fresh fruit and vegetables by age indicates that age groups over 45 are the main consumers, eating more than twice the amount that the under 25 group consumes.[4]

Until recently there have been no true producer-only farmers' markets operating in the UK, so there is little specific consumer profile information available. Insights into consumer profiles can be obtained from research on similar direct food marketing outlets such as farm shops. Findings indicating that UK farm shop customers are likely to be female, upper income and middle aged are similar to findings in the US, Japan and Germany. These customers are regular purchasers but also buy at supermarkets. Shopping habits appear to be flexible, suggesting that they are self employed or housewives or pensioners, an assumption which is backed up by American research. (See H. Festing.[11])

A small survey carried out at the street market in Glastonbury gave credence to H. Festing's conclusions in that, for example, 70% of buyers of organic produce in the market purchased other goods including fruit and vegetables from supermarkets. 84% of purchasers said that they wished to buy directly from the producer because they wished to promote local business and that the food was cheaper and fresher (in that order).

At the Bath farmers' market, survey results indicate that 55% of customers were over 40 and that they purchased goods from the market because the food was freshly harvested (47%) and was good quality (45%). Furthermore 38% of customers purchased food because it was direct from the producer. A similar percentage also said that they liked to support local business.[15]

9. The market managers

Council-operated markets and private street market operators are represented by their own national associations and both are concerned at the decline in market business due to out-of-town supermarkets. They work with government planners in reviewing planning permission criteria for new out-of-town developments and their implications for inner city decline.

Other problems that the associations see are:

- Restrictions of environmental health regulations.
- Poor public transport and/or poor parking. As many traditional markets are sited in the centre of towns, parking inevitably becomes a problem as customers do not wish to carry large quantities of fresh produce any distance.
- Need for better legislation on car boot sales
- Poor public image of street markets due to problems from a minority of privately operated markets. The national association has a membership of 17 major companies but there are a total of 300 private operators plus an unknown number of illegal operators. Until legislation controls all such operations the poor image given to street markets by the few illegal operators will continue.
- No reinvestment by councils of the markets' operating profits.

Bath Farmers' Market.

5 Points arising from the UK case studies

There have been a number of market initiatives around the UK by a range of interested organisations which have had mixed success.

- *The Bath Market* (see Chapter 4). This is still at the pilot stage and its development is to be closely followed.
- *The Spitalfields Organic Market* (see Chapter 3). This has been established for five and a half years and operates as a market within a market.
- *The Barnstaple Pannier Market* (see Chapter 3). An old established market reinvigorated in the 1980s.
- *The Knowsley initiative* (see Chapter 4). This market is still in the planning stage

There is no common thread to the way each of these markets has been developed. It is interesting that the approaches that have been tried in the UK are all different. The Bath market started from scratch whereas the Spitalfields and Barnstaple markets developed successfully out of an existing regular market. In contrast the Knowsley market which was to start from scratch has not progressed beyond the planning stages.

The costs to the seller

In order to recruit producers to participate in a new market, they will need to be assured of the returns they can expect for the effort put in. Costings for the Knowlesy and Bath projects are summarised below:

Suggested costings to run a stall at a farmers' market

Item	1	2	3	4
sales	750	200	300	300
profit on return (as % of sales)	188	100	75	75
transport (40 miles @ 50p)	20	20	20	20
market promotion and organisation/stall	35	n/a*	n/a*	20+13
stall fees	12	5	10	20
total costs	67	25	30	73
margin	121	75	45	2
returns per hour	£5.04	£4.68	£1.87	£0.08

* covered by Bath and North-East Somerset Council budget

1. *Illustrative budget prepared for Knowsley project*[17]
- A profit on return basis of 25% has been used which is applicable to commercial retailers.
- Two people are needed to run the stall (8x2=16 hours) plus 4 hrs work to get ready and 4 hours to pack up, hence the 24 hours quoted. Two tables are required.

2. *Bath local grower*
- A profit on return basis of 50% sales
- A smallholder would only spend 16 hours on market duties if only 1 person runs the stall. In this case only one table is necessary.

3. *Bath stallholder with average returns*
- A profit on return basis of 25%.
- 2 people are needed to run the stall (8x2=16hrs) plus 4 hours work to get ready and 4 hours to pack up, hence the 24 hours quoted. Two tables are required.

4. *Average Bath stallholder including start-up costs*
- Total start-up costs of £13,500 offset over 24 markets (1 year) between 42 stalls (max. capacity) is £13/stall.
- The regular promotion/organisation costs for the Bath market are estimated at £588/market amongst 30 stallholders or £20 each.
- Stallholder will require 2 stalls at £10 each.

These figures show how financially marginal newly established markets like these can be. To produce a return of £5/hr the producer at Bath for example would have had to achieve sales of £600, a figure which was only achieved at Bath by three commercial high value produce stallholders (selling smoked meat and cheese). The producer with the average income at Bath of £300 and a return on revenue of 25% would barely have justified his/her time and effort.

It is of course questionable whether these calculations are relevant to the small-scale producer whose profit margin would be more like 50% of revenue instead of 25%, giving a return of £4.68/hr. Similarly the increased financial viability that commercial producers gain when increasing the profit on return percentage presents a more positive picture (e.g. at Bath the producer's returns/hr increases to £5.00 for a 50% profit on return).

It is important to note that the total start-up costs spread over the three markets would be the equivalent of £107/stall and so no producer is going to be eager to participate for solely financial reasons unless the start-up costs are already funded.

Despite these low returns on input, commercial traders were still keen to participate in the Bath farmers' market. It is the indirect benefits that are hard to quantify, such as raising their public profile and personal contact with customers, that financially justify their continuing presence.

The success of Spitalfields and Barnstaple farmers' markets has been partly due to the fact that they have not had the high start-up costs although Spitalfields did have promotional costs that had to be offset over the first 18 operating months.

The type of producer

There are two types of producer that may participate in a farmers' market. One is the established commercial producer with at least one or two existing retail outlets. This producer is interested in diversifying marketing outlets and will be looking primarily at the profitability of a particular outlet. Then there is the part time or backyard producer who is looking to establish a regular business and regards the farmers' market as a low cost marketing outlet that may give an initial opportunity to test the market potential. Mostly this is his or her only formal retail outlet. At the Bath market there was a mix of sellers with 40% selling only through farm shops and wholesalers and 60% selling at least some their produce informally in direct sales outlets. A survey of Californian farmers' market sellers also showed this mix, with products being sold to packers (22%) and wholesalers (21%) and 55% to other direct marketing outlets.[16]

Large-scale producers regard a day's marketing as an expensive exercise in time and need a large turnover to justify their presence. At Bath these sellers were experienced in their approach to selling and gave the newly established market a professional air which reassured some of the shoppers. They were motivated more by the chance of promoting their produce and stimulating existing outlets than by profit on the day. There were also smallholders who perhaps did not value their time fully and were happy to attend and earn some money from their vegetable plots. It was these farmers that gave the market its local and social atmosphere. There is a danger that if only the professional 'farm shop' type of producer is present the market is too upmarket to attract regular shoppers who feel that prices are inflated and the market is a niche speciality market (which works well for annual food fairs such as Ludlow). Shoppers will come to this type of market at first but once the novelty wears off fewer people will attend.

Thus as the aspirations of the two types of producers are different they need to be specifically targeted when recruiting for a market. As seen above, as long as the start-up costs are covered a small-scale producer will be happy with the potential returns whereas it is more marginal for commercially orientated producers. In these cases it is necessary to investigate the hidden benefits which cannot be priced — as the following case study of the cheesemaker illustrates.

• •

A Bath cheesemaker

A commercial cheese seller at the Bath market was reluctant to participate as his cheeses were expensive at £3.50 each and he was concerned that his local retail outlets in Bath would object to him undercutting their retail prices. Thus he was obliged to sell at the full price. He came prepared to show the customers how the cheeses were made and was able to show each individual step on his stall. In the course of the first market he sold out of all 200 cheeses that he brought with him. Not only did he succeed in selling more produce but he found his regular retail outlets reported customers asking specifically for his cheeses, thus boosting sales.

• •

Funding

Producers will only participate if at least the start-up costs are covered by someone. EU 'Objective 5b funding' or local council subsidies have been sought or used for the Knowsley and Bath markets. Certainly the Bath initiative would probably not have got beyond the planning stage without the council input.

The success of obtaining funding will however depend on the potential beneficiaries, and a more convincing argument can be made for funding where a range of potential benefits can be seen, for example inner city development with social and community development benefits, plus assistance to low income marginal rural farmers, rather than seeking subsidies for farmers' markets that are solely aimed at helping established farming enterprises to diversify.

Fresh apple juice at Bath Farmers' Market.

6 Critical factors that make or break a farmers' market

1. Balance of categories of produce

A market that has a long line of local producers all selling tomatoes will not bring in the custom. The producers themselves won't be too happy due to the competition. Care has to be taken that there is a balance not only within a product category but also between categories. Shoppers do not only want to buy vegetables but, for example, meat, baked goods, dairy products and even flowers.

Goods for sale	Number of stalls	
	Ludlow market	Bath farmers' market
Fruit and vegetables	9	9
Plants and shrubs	3	2
Clothing	3	0
Crafts	4	1
Antiques	3	0
Jewellery	2	0
Books	1	0
Dairy produce	4	3
Meat	1	3
Beer, wine, juice	2	4
Baked goods	3	2
Processed goods	6	2

Farmers' markets cannot compete with supermarket 'one stop shopping' concepts but they need to aspire to the idea as much as possible. The allocation of stalls at the Barnstaple market (see Chapter 3) was, according to the manager, a critical decision in revitalising the market in the early 1970s when the market was dominated by clothing stalls. Some competition between stallholders is welcome although competitors normally adjust their product range to reduce these problems (e.g. plant sellers select niche markets selling ornamentals separately from rare plants and alpines).

2. Critical number of stalls

It is important to have sufficient stalls to attract attention and if the market is to be fully commercial the income from the stallholders (typically £15-20/stall/day) must be sufficient to pay the costs of the market including management. Many farmers' markets in California for example have only 10 stalls but these are part of a federation of markets in the immediate area and so advertising and promotion costs are shared. These markets also operate outside in car parks and so have few running costs. This is more of a problem in the UK where the weather will play a decisive role in customer attendance.

Market	No. of stalls	Cost per stall per day
Bristol French Market	24	£12 - £15
Bath Farmers Market	30	£5*
Ludlow Market	43	£12
Spitalfields organic market	12	£30
Barnstaple pannier market	300	£1.60 equivalent
R&C street market	30	£15 - £20

* Subsidised rate

Experience at the Bath farmers' market suggests that at least 25 stalls are required if the market is to attract sufficient customers as well as keeping the stall rental charge down to a reasonable level. Problems can arise when, due to insufficient producers coming forward, markets allow non-producers to dominate. This immediately changes the character of the market and the expectations of the customers.

3. Professional *vs* part-time sellers

Both the produce and the sellers in a farmers' market should make a good impression on prospective customers. Thus apart from the range of goods on sale there needs to be a range of types of seller. A mix of professional producer sellers and back garden/allotment sellers is required in order to give the impression that the market is a community effort and has a social atmosphere. By attracting commercial producers with experience in running farm shops, a market can be assured of a professional approach to selling that can help it to operate for the good of part time producers.

4. Quality of produce

It is critical that produce on sale is of the best quality. 45% of Bath farmers' market customers gave quality of food as the main reason for shopping at the market. This is what customers have told farmers' market organisers in the USA. Sommer[1] reports that 63% of customers at farmers' markets in California put food quality as the most important reason for buying at farmers' markets. Overripe fruit or badly marked vegetables will give the impression of cheap goods that customers associate with failing street markets. Produce on sale should be of the standard that customers expect from supermarkets but fresher and cheaper due to the reduced overheads.

5. Good publicity

The value of good publicity when starting a farmers' market cannot be overstated. The full range of advertisements and publicity outlets should be exploited
- Fliers that are placed in public places, doctors waiting rooms, libraries etc.
- Local radio and television. Participating farmers should be recruited for interviews.
- Local newspapers and free sheets.
- Newsletters of interested local groups.
- The organisers and producers should be prepared to visit local group meetings to give talks on the ideas behind the markets.

6. Identify main role of market

It is important at the outset when setting up a farmers' market to identify the main purpose of establishing the market. Is it primarily to stimulate the economy of an inner city area or is it to give farmers an alternative retail outlet? For example, an application for funding assistance will depend on the target beneficiaries — as in EU Objective 5b for rural diversification, or Objective 1 for social development. The balance of stallholders and what they sell would need to be geared to meet the requirements of the prospective customers.

7. Farmers' market regulations

A key issue is the imposition of farmers' market regulations on the participants. Invariably, when these markets are started few rules or regulations are necessary. However, as the markets become more successful with more disparate sellers there is a need for more regulations. The way in which the market is operated and for whom it is operated will underpin its success.

The structure of the organisation must be laid out clearly as a legal document so as to avoid any future disputes between stallholders. Markets can be organised as associations with the need for paid up members who vote for an executive committee who then employ a market manager to run the market. The certified farmers' markets in California operate within an association structure with its own standard code of practice that is legally binding.

There is a need to certify producer sellers if the public are to accept the concept of a producer–only market, but this means there must be some way of policing the certification. The Soil Association and other organisations have established an organic certification process in the UK and a similar process for bona fide local producers will need to be followed if credence in these markets is to be maintained. The agricultural extension service in Greece for example carry out this service for their markets but there is not an equivalent organisation that could do this in the UK. This role will have to be undertaken by the market management.

• •

Secondary certification in Californian farmers' markets

Until recently certified Californian farmers' markets regulations permitted farmers to sell other farmers' produce in conjunction with their own if they applied to the market authorities for secondary certificates. These authorised a named farmer to sell produce belonging to two other certified producers at any one time. He could thus sell produce from a range of farmers through the year and benefit from the seasonality of production of farmers in different climatic zones. This also allowed farmers to have their produce sold at different markets on the same day.

This regulation started to be abused but was driven by the consumer demand for a variety of produce to be available. 17% of sellers in the Santa Barbara farmers' market were selling produce under secondary certificates and at some markets the proportion was as high as 70%.

This rule has now been changed after a vituperative court hearing costing the Santa Barbara farmers' market board $30,000 in lawyers' fees. Farmers are now allowed to sell bought-in produce from only one farmer at a time and produce must be displayed separately and must not amount to more than half of the produce on the stall. It must also be separately labelled.

Source: 'We are not a supermarket' *Farmers' Market Monthly*, May 1996[12]

• •

Organic regulations

There is a specific need for some basic regulations concerning the differentiation of certified organic produce from other 'unsprayed', 'chemical free' or 'in conversion' produce. It is important that sellers of non-certified produce do not mislead the public by using the word 'organic' and efforts should be made at the markets to educate the public on the organic certification standards. The organic certification bodies in the UK must play a leading role in this. Market managers should be careful that produce sellers' claims of 'unsprayed produce' are fully justified by making unscheduled visits to farms as necessary. Permission to do this must be laid out in the market regulations.

8. Trading regulations

A wide range of both national and local council regulatory bodies are involved with the establishment of a farmers' market. These include:

- Local council planning department — Is concerned with site permission to hold a market and to erect banners and advertising.
- Environmental health section — There are controls over the handling and transport of food to be sold as outlined in the Food Hygiene (General) Regulations 1970 and the Food Safety Act 1990. Anyone operating a food retail business must seek registration and undergo inspection by an environmental health officer.
- Trading standards section — The accuracy of weighing scales must be tested and all labelling of produce should be clear and accurate.
- Highways department — Permission for street closures or operating on a public highway or path must be sought through this body.
- Licensing section — Licenses for street trading and entertainments

must be obtained.

- Magistrates' court — A temporary licence to sell alcoholic drinks must be obtained through these courts. It is a requirement that at least one stallholder has a full 'on-licence' before a temporary licence is issued.
- Fire department — It is advisable to consult with the local fire department to ensure that all fire regulations are being complied with.

9. Training

If farmers and other producers are going to sell produce direct to the public successfully they have to learn to be good shopkeepers and be prepared to invest in the necessary training. They must learn how to present their produce as well as how best to deal with the public. Farmer organisations must take on this role if the farmers are to benefit fully from the opportunities that farmers' markets can offer. Organisations such as the Farm Retail Association and National Farmers' Union currently assist their members on this issue.

Training on health and safety measures can be organised through the Chartered Institute of Environmental Health who run basic hygiene courses with six hours of tuition that could be orientated specifically to sellers in farmers' markets.

10. Entertainment

A distinguishing feature of farmers' markets when compared to regular street markets is entertainment. A key role of the market manager is to recruit and programme entertainment that is:

- Not static — Clowns or jugglers moving amongst the crowds are better than performances in one place that stop the crowds and cause 'traffic jams' amongst the stalls, reducing customer throughput.
- Appeals to a wide range of customers — The customers wish to enjoy their visit to the market and not all music for example is to everyone's taste: thus a range of music should be on offer. If a market study of the customers reveals special characteristics (e.g. 60% aged over 60) then entertainment can be geared to this clientele. If there are a number of families visiting, children's puppet shows or even a sectioned off crèche will be an attraction.
- Is not overbearing or too loud — Amplified music is not recommended unless in a large market. The music should be seen as a complement to the atmosphere and not the dominating influence.

Children's entertainment at Bath Farmers' Market

- Is not too costly — The cost of all the entertainment needs to be split amongst all stallholders and, as outlined in Chapter 5 in the analysis of costs, market overheads need to be carefully controlled.
- Does not take up a lot of space — In order to keep the overhead costs to the stallholders to a minimum all available space must be allocated to stallholders: thus any stage or platform for entertainment is a potential lost stall site.
- Varied — If the market is a regular event customers don't want to see the same acts week after week. Cooking demonstrations, free tastings and seasonal events should be scheduled.

One answer is to recruit good local buskers and allocate specific spaces for them. But there are problems that can outweigh the benefits; for instance, depending on the site of the market, street licences may be necessary and customers do not like to be hustled for money. If entertainers are employed, at least the manager has full control over location and the quality of the entertainment.

Media coverage - Bath Farmers' Market.

7 The way forward

If farmers' markets are to become successfully established in the UK, a number of points must be considered.

1 The success of farmers' markets in the USA has been due to the large number of smallholders that are in production and the support they receive from the public and government subsidised agricultural extension services. The UK Agricultural Development and Advisory Service (ADAS) is run as a commercial operation charging commercial consultancy rates for their advice. Smallholders on their own cannot afford these fees and must organise themselves collectively to seek assistance. The UK does not have such numbers of smallholders as are needed to supply this type of market except in a limited number of areas. Where there are not the numbers of smallholders the way forward would be to look again at the existing types of markets and to adapt them rather than establishing new genuine farmers' markets. For example, areas could be set aside in street or covered markets specifically for producer-only stalls. This could be seen as a way of revitalising these types of market. Specific promotional efforts would need to made in these cases.

2 Farmers' markets have a lot to learn from supermarkets and the reasons for their success. There are benefits on both sides if a farmers' market were to be established alongside a supermarket. Many farmers' markets in the USA are established on supermarket car parks. These markets are not seen as competition but rather as an added attraction. Customers will patronise both premises as they cannot buy all their requirements in the farmers' markets.

3 Where funding is limited it may be preferable to concentrate efforts on helping new smallholders to supply farmers' markets rather than encouraging producers with established market outlets. New farmers will be

more flexible and adaptable in their marketing approach and more likely to direct most if not all of their production to the market. They are more likely to show an immediate profit by selling at these markets.

4 As more feedback about the customers at farmers' markets becomes available in the UK it will be possible to gear the markets towards the profile of the predominant type of customer. It is already known that the customer is typically over 40 years old, lives locally and most likely female, although families are common. Thus location of the market close to areas where these people are living is important. Advertising and market entertainment could be directed specifically at these customers.

5 As seen in the USA, agricultural extension advice to producers has been important in maintaining the numbers of participating farmers and the volume of produce for the markets. Assistance to new producers and training in both production techniques and marketing skills will be important. There are a range of producer organisations that will need to react to their members' interest in farmers' markets.

6 In order to get a good range of produce on sale at the market, contacts with a wide range of local producers and their representative organisations will be needed. This can only be done effectively by local organisers. The stimulus for farmers' markets may come from outside the community but the implementation will best be carried out by local producers and consumers.

7 How markets are managed will need to be flexible. The way that associations of market sellers operate in the USA may well be unsuited to the UK. When markets are in the early stages of establishment the adoption of rules and regulations must be on a provisional basis as it would be easy for a group of successful participants to gear regulations to their own short-term benefit. A democratic approach must take into account the opportunities for newcomers (who may be potential competition) to the market. Decision makers must understand the importance of the three critical factors in the long term success of farmers' markets:
- maintaining a range of both commercial and semi-commercial or part time producers;
- only producers are allowed to sell;
- only locally produced and processed goods are on sale.

Useful addresses

The Soil Association, 86 Colston Street, Bristol BS1 5BB
The Farming and Rural Conservation Agency, Woodthorne, Wergs Road, Wolverhampton WV6 8TQ
The Farm Retail Association, 164 Shaftesbury Avenue, London WC2H 8HL
The National Association of British Market Authorities, NBMA House, 21 Tarnside Road, Orrell, Wigan WN5 8RN
WI Country Markets Ltd., Reada House, Vachel Road, Reading RG1 1NY
British Speciality Foods, Food from Britain, 123 Buckingham Palace Road, London SW1W 9SA
The National Society of Allotment and Leisure Gardeners Ltd., O'Dell House, Hunters Road, Corby NN17 5JE
Safe Alliance, 38 Ebury Street, London SW1W 0LU
National Food Alliance, 5–11 Worship Street, London EC2A 2BE
Women's Environmental Network, 87 Worship Street, London EC2A 2BE
National Federation of City Farms, The Greenhouse, Hereford Street, Bedminster, Bristol BS3 4NA
National Farmers' Union, Agriculture House, 164 Shaftesbury Avenue, London WC2H 8HL

References

1   R. Sommer. (1980): Direct Marketing Project. *Public Service Research Review.*

2   USDA Farmers' Market Survey Report 1995 and 1996.

3   *Farmers' Markets and Rural Economic Development.* Community Agric. Dev. Series by Dept. of Rural Sociology, Cornell University.

4   J. Farbstein & R. Wener: *Connections: Creating Urban Excellence* 1991.

5   H. Festing : *Direct Marketing of Fresh Produce* 1995.

6   Brun and Echinard 1989: as quoted by H. Festing in 5 above.

7   Merkl 1989 and Brun and Echinard 1989 as quoted by H. Festing in 5 above.

8   Cornell University Coop Extension funding proposal 1994.

9   'In Search of Food Security'. Morris Newman 1997 Internet.

10 Hess 1974: as quoted by R. Sommer in 'Farmers' Markets as Community Events' in *Public Places and Spaces* eds Altman & Zube. 1989.

11 As quoted by H. Festing in 'The potential for direct marketing by small farms in the UK' *Farm Management* Vol.9 No.8 1996/7.

12 'We are not a Supermarket' *Farmers' Market Monthly.* May 1996.

13 Nordin C.: International Public Market Conf. 1996.

14 S. Vaupel: 'Marketing Organic Produce in Certified Farmers' Markets'. *Small Farm News* March 1991.

15 S. Vaupel: *Who sells at urban farmers' markets.* University of Calif. Davis 1987.

For further information about the Local Food Links
Project, contact
The Soil Association
86/88 Colston Street
Bristol BS1 5BB
Tel 0117 929 0661
Fax 0117 925 2504

Notes